# Snapshots From God

Sandy Szymanski

xulon
PRESS

17-1306

To Monica !

Always remember
God is there waiting
for you

Love
Aunt
Lonby

Heb 13:2

# Orchestra of God

*E*very aspect of the sky was shown as my friend and I walked the beach that morning to catch the sunrise. We saw only rays peek from between the gray clouds that persisted as they moved away from the rising sun. Finally we saw the sun as it showed its wonder in the bright blue sky. Just as suddenly, though, a cloud covered it from another direction.

Looking to the west, as we finally started back, the island of Sanibel was still clear, the lighthouse was still flashing it's warning light. The sun was now shining in a baby blue sky it was going to be a beautiful day.

As we sat on a bench watching the birds hop around on the sea oats, we didn't notice the change. An enormous thunderhead, so brilliant white it was dazzling, appeared with a broken rainbow, with feathery straggly, gray clouds floating past determined to cover it. The breeze was just as determined to move the clouds away. We then decided to walk to the end of the island; the thunderhead followed us with the broken rainbow showing up in different area's, but always there. As we got to the end of the island, out in the distance Sanibel Island was now completely shrouded with dark clouds, and rain was quickly moving in on us. With the sun to our back, shining brightly, who would win the sun or the rain? It is always a toss up on the beach. Turning back to the car, the drops of rain started gently to fall. In the end they pelted us, the rain had started in earnest.

The beautiful morning had turned into a rainstorm. For some it ruined their days but for me it showed a wonderful performance of God's beauty as we watched Him orchestrate the heavenly firmament around to show his awesomeness. We left soaking wet, but considering it was all worth it to see God's show.

**Psalm 8:1**
O Lord our Lord, how majestic is your name in all the earth! You have set your glory above the heavens.

**Psalm 65:5**
You answer us with awesome deeds of righteousness, O God our Savior, the hope of all the ends of the earth and of the farthest seas,

# The Wonder Of It All

*T*he single drop of rain hanging from a leaf like a diamond
The exquisite web of a spider done up as a piece of lace in
the early morning dew. The unexpected chirping of a cardinal dancing from limb to limb in a tree. The only sound that is made. A frag-
ile rosebud on a bush once thought dead. The wonder of it all. Is
there any reason not to believe and trust in the one who has done all
of this for us? His morning gifts how many of us see. In such a
hurry we pass them by, if God could make the heavens and the earth
for us to enjoy why don't we? Genesis 1:10 says and God saw that
it was good. Actually that line is mentioned three times and the
fourth time it says it was very good. I think it would be very good
for us to enjoy what he has given us. It is his good morning gift to
us every day.

**Genesis 1:10**
it says: and God saw that it was good.
Actually that line is mentioned three times and the fourth time it
says it was very good. I think it would be very good for us to enjoy
what he has given us. It is his good morning gift to us every day.

**LAMENTATIONS 3: 22-23**
Because of his great love we are not consumed, for his compassions
never fail they are new every morning. Great is your faithfulness

**Genesis 1:14**

And God said, "Let there be lights in the expanse of the sky to separate the day from the night, and to let them serve as a signs to mark seasons and days and years,

# A Holy Mess

☫

Some days we just can't seem to get it together. No matter how hard we try. Nothing seems to fall in place. We wake up **late, spill** our coffee, pour **too much** cereal, we leave **late** for work **hit** every **red light.** People **pull out** in front of us. Nothing seems to fall into place. When we get to work, someone says how are you today and you reply "I'm just a mess today" nothing is going right for me. I wish I could have stayed in bed all day today. Well we are a mess when Jesus gets hold of us. He straightens us out, sets us on the right path and guides us, so we are no longer the mess he found us in. We will still have our moments but He will be there to guide us.

**Romans 8:26**
In the same way, the Spirit helps us in our weakness.

**Proverbs 18:24** A man of many companions may come to ruin, but there is a friend who sticks closer than a brother.

# Morning Call

I love the early morning,
The morning star in the east disappears as the faint blush
of dawn starts to appear
The nighttime quiet gives way to early morning music
The butterflies already showing their beauty
The birds starting their serenades to start the day,
listen closely, you can hear the different types.
The morning dew as it drips steadily from the trees.
The vast array of colors that herald the early dawn
I see the sun coming up and the earth coming alive
Sunrise must be God's favorite time of day

**Jeremiah 33:3**
Call to me and I will answer you and tell you great and unsearchable
things you do not know.

**Psalm 143:8**
Let the morning bring me word of your unfailing love, for I have
put my trust in you. Show me the way I should go, for to you I lift
up my soul.

# Sheer Beauty

As our cruise ship silently glided into Yukatat Bay we saw it from a distance, the majestic Hubbard Glacier. The morning sun sending glistening diamonds as it shined on it. Sounding like gunfire the shots rang out. We didn't know where to look as the thunder followed. All of a sudden, right in front of us, a massive wall of ice just slid right down the glacier as if it had been oiled. Majestically it cascaded into the water barely making a ripple effect. The boomerang effect of other smaller calving followed as we continued to just be in awe. The beauty of the glacier calving will be forever etched in my mind as one of the most beautiful things of God's creation. You never know when it is going to happen but when it does, it is a show to behold; no description can accurately tell you what it is like. You have to see it to believe it.

**Job 38:18**
Have you comprehended the vast expanse of the earth? Tell me if you know all of this.

# To My Grandchild

My prayers for you as you arrive.
A healthy life. A love for God.
Crawling, creeping, sitting walking,
Through all of life's stages,
A steady stream of God's love will flow.
From the generic words of:
"Now I lay me down to sleep."
To your more personal words of love and faith.
Learn what your parents teach.
Let people see you as being
Loving, generous, kind.
Never selfish or ugly.
Always have a smile on your face.
It takes more muscles to frown than to smile.
Put God first in all that you do for
He will make your paths straight.
Love your grandparents, as different as they all are,
For you will learn a life's lesson from all of them.
Try never to hurt your Momma
For those wounds
go deep, they take years to heal.
Love your Momma with all your heart.
Be friends with your Daddy go fishing,
Go to football games,
Watch cartoons together,

Play trucks and cars.
Love your Daddy with all your heart.
Gazing at my baby holding her baby.
These are the things I pray for you
As I hold you for the very first time.

Dedicated to Ethan born 7-9-03

**Proverbs 22:6**
Train a child in the way he should go, and when he is old he will not turn away from it.

**Ephesians 6:1, 2**
Children, obey your parents in the Lord, for this is right. Honor your father and mother which is the first commandment with a promise

# *Drifting Clouds*

*I* see the quarter moon trying to shine as the clouds drift lazily by. Playing hide and seek, with a silver lining as the clouds drift lazily by. Early dawn trying to creep in. But all I see are lazy drifting clouds. The moon is in the west, finally trying to set. The sun in the east vainly trying to rise, but all I see are lazy drifting clouds scattered in all directions.

Lazy drifting clouds are something we should be able to associate with. We get lazy and don't know what we want to do. We sleep in and a whole day goes by. We have done nothing. Drifting in and out of the day, not motivated to do anything, just being lazy.

In proverbs, the lazy sluggard is the same way. We must be careful or the enemy will slip in and shoot his fiery darts, being lazy and not motivated is a tool of the devils. Don't fall for it.

We should look to the ant who stocks up for the winter and hard times.

**Proverbs 6:9-11**
How long will you lay there, you sluggard? When will you get up from your sleep? A little sleep, a little slumber, a little folding of the hands to rest and poverty will come on you like a bandit.

**Proverb 30:25**
Ants are creatures of little strength, yet they store up their food in the summer;

# God's Scrub Brush!

*E*ver feel like God is scrubbing you? While doing my morning prayers I was praying, asking God to continue to purge me and make me clean. All of a sudden, an image of a red handled scrub brush came to mind. After working in the yard, dirty from head to foot from pulling weeds and raking, we go inside to take a shower. We use the scrub brush to scrub our bodies and stubborn dirt from under our fingernails. Isn't that just like God, to take his scrub brush, scrub us up nice and clean and rinse us in Living Water. The plant hyssop symbolized spiritual purity. Let us always remember that we are God's creation for Him to scrub and clean up.

**Psalm 51:7**
Cleanse me with hyssop, and I will be clean; wash me, and I will be whiter than snow.

# God's Cleansing

While browsing at the pictures of the devastation that hurricane Isabel had dealt the eastern seaboard, I had to stop and think of God's majesty. His awesome powers shown in the waves as they crashed over the shores onto roads to turn them into useless places filled with water. I could only imagine in my mind the howling and screeching of the wind as it ripped apart peoples homes, boats; trees that were years and years old thrown around as if they were now toothpicks. The mightiness of God showing his powers. The beaches of North Carolina and South Carolina will never be the same. When we accept Jesus Christ into our lives his love sweeps thru us like the winds of a hurricane. We are cleansed like the rain that cleansed after the fury. His mighty whirlwinds of love wrap us with forgiveness. We will never be the same again. Just like the shores of those beaches. We are forever changed, forever cleansed.

**Psalm 57:1**
Have mercy on me O God, have mercy on me, for in you my soul takes refuge. I will take refuge in the shadow of your wings until the disaster has passed.

# On the Job Training 101

Studying the bible as children of Christ, we should all want to learn. At our jobs we do all we can to learn to make a good impression on our bosses. We use the dictionaries; we ask questions and generally show a great interest in everything around. In the New Testament, Paul tells Timothy to study to show himself approved. De we use all the resources that are available to us to study God's word? Remember He gave it to us to follow as a handbook. Yet we are afraid to ask questions because we might appear as if we are not smart. We don't study the commentaries or use the concordance (they are too big or too bulky) a devotional or maybe not even go to church. We don't or won't take the time to look up words that are in the dictionary or the concordance to find the exact meaning of difficult words. Although we have so many tools at hand to help us. With computer technology at our fingertips, we can click into any resource we need. The book of Deuteronomy is full of instructions for us. Let's use the resources that God gave us and not just scratch the surface. So God can say to us someday "well done good and faithful servant."

**Job 6:24**
Teach me and I will be quiet, show me where I have been wrong.

**Exodus 4:12**
Now go I will teach you…

# Knowledge is Not Enough

Constant everyday reading, studying my bible, devotions, bible study and going to church, it all looked good. Still there was something missing, there was a tugging there that I could not explain. I felt I was right with God. I was doing all the right things. Isn't that what he wants from us? After a conversation with a friend of mine, I noticed that she had grown tremendously in the Lord in the past year. I asked her what was her secret. Falling in love with Jesus was her answer. It was then I realized I wanted what she had. I wanted more. More than I thought I could give. I started spending time with her, asking questions. I was hungry. I started to pray differently, studied my bible in a new way. I asked questions of her and others. I was headed into the right direction, just taking a detour. After having talked with her and asking questions I have developed a much closer and deeper relationship with Jesus. Words cannot describe how I feel now. Spending time with Jesus, talking with and asking him to teach me. What a brand new outlook on life I have now. Everyday has new perspective to it. Jesus is in charge. I try to keep him in my uppermost thoughts all day long and the last thing at night. I now want all I can get out of my relationship with Jesus through my studying and reading.

**Jeremiah 20:9**
His word is in my heart like a fire, shut up in my bones.

# Dress Rehearsal

*P*ractice makes perfect or so they say. I wonder what we will be like in heaven??

It's always being said that we are practicing here on earth. I am so glad.

We sing in church, dance when we are rejoicing and praising in the Lord, clap our hands use instruments. Boy! I need a lot of rehearsal. I can't carry a tune; I can only make a joyful noise, and dancing like Miriam and the women did in the dessert, forget it!! I have two left feet. I can't clap in time and I am an utter disaster with a tambourine. When we get to heaven, though we will be singing like the angels on high. We will be floating on the clouds, dancing all the time. Instruments will be in perfect harmony. Never feel embarrassed about how you sing, dance, clap your hands or even sway to the music. Remember you are performing for your Lord Jesus. He loves us in spite of our imperfections and we are only practicing for the big day in heaven when we stand in front of Him and give our all and all.

**Psalm 108:1**
My heart is steadfast, O God; I will sing and make music with all my soul.

**Exodus 15:20**
Then Miriam the prophetess, Aaron's sister, took a tambourine in her hand, and all the women followed her, with tambourines and dancing.

# Mashed Potatoes
# and Gravy

*A* re you truly hungry for God? When we are in the valley and really feeling low we discover our plate is empty. We are hungry and sometimes we have to search to see exactly what we are hungry for. We discover that we are hungry for God and his love. My favorite vegetable is mashed potatoes and gravy, any kind of gravy, but it had to be real mashed potatoes. I always remember the milk gravy my mom used to make with fried chicken, creamy milk gravy with all the greasy crumbs in it from the fried chicken. I would also mix in my corn at the same time. That was always so good. After one helping I always desired more. With God we want to always have that craving desire for more. More mashed potatoes and gravy please. Also known as wanting more of God.

**Matthew 5:6**
Blessed are those who hunger and thirst after righteousness, for they will be filled.

**Psalm 34:8**
Taste and see that the Lord is good.

**Psalm 38:9**
All my longings lie open before you, O Lord; my sighing is not hidden from you.

# Complaining

*T*he book of Job is the story of this man and his friends after God allows Satan to test Job.

So many times we focus on the fact of Job's patience. We hear the expression " you have the patience of Job," well if you continue through to the end of the book you will find this magnificent chapter, it is a gem of a chapter, Chapter 38, when God answers Job out of the whirlwind of how he created the earth. What a magnificent description. Could this be why I have such a love for his creation? The angels were all there to see it burst forth at God's command. So? Why don't we enjoy it? Seems all people do is complain about it. Too hot, too cold, too humid, looks like rain, too much rain. Ice, snow, snowed under, snowed in. You name it and they complain about the weather. I cannot even imagine the sky looking any other way and the weather being any different than the way God made it. He created the sunshine, the rainbows, and the beautiful clouds. In the book of Exodus that is all the Israelites did was complain. They did it all the time. There is a lesson here for us. Stop your whining and complaining. Enjoy God's creation. I am sure he did not make it for us to complain about.

**Psalm 37:4**
Delight yourself in the Lord and He will give you the desires of your heart.

# Quiet Sunrise

Gray clouds covering the dawn,
Looking dark and dreary.
Is it going to rain?
Will the sun break through and shine?
The morning birds are quiet to sing or not to sing?
On the horizon faint pale gold appears
Showing the day arriving.
The questions are all gone


Let the sleep leave your eyes.
Welcome Jesus into your day.
He will help you cope in everything you do.
Just look to Him the Son has risen!


**Gen 1:3**
And God said, let there be light, and there was light.

**John 1:4,5**
In Him was life, and that life was the light of men.

The light shines in the darkness, but the darkness has not understood it.

# What are you afraid of?

We are always being challenged to step out of our comfort zones. Yet we are afraid. We use the excuse; too old, too busy, I will fail, I am just not smart enough. How do we know until we try? We are never too old to learn something new. **Too old?** Look at Moses, he lead the Israelites out of Egypt when he was 80 years old. **Not smart enough?** Jesus chose some of his disciples who were just fishermen. **Fear of failure?** Look at Simon Peter, he failed the ultimate test, yet recovered and became a writer of two of the books of the New Testament (with the help of the Holy Spirit) and most of all the leader of the church. We will never know unless we try, who else thinks we are not smart enough, with your heavenly Father's help you can achieve anything you want. **Try!** Slip out of that comfort zone and try something new. As it says in the book " let not your heart be troubled." Set out to do something you want to achieve. It says in Corinthians "I can do all things through Christ who strengthens me. Step out Accomplish something brand new.

**2 Corinthians 12:10**
that is why for Christ's sake, I delight in weaknesses, in insults, in hardships, in persecutions, in difficulties. For when I am weak, then I am strong.

# *Salt*

*I*n Mathew 5:13 it says we are the salt of the earth. Salt makes food taste better that is why it is added in all packaged foods and in our diets. Crunchy French Fries taste better with salt, along with popcorn, potato chips, and pretzels and other salty items. We should flavor other people's lives with our witness as our salt. We can flavor their day by helping them, telling them good morning, telling them they look good that day. Don't be grouchy. In general, just being warm and friendly. Leviticus 2:13 says they added salt to their grain offerings, so this an old testament command. While in this modern world we are told to leave the salt off of those crunchy French fries, lets add salt to our personalities.

**Colossians 4:6**
Let your conversations be always full of grace, seasoned with salt, so that you may know how to answer everyone.

**Ephesians 4:29**
Do not let any unwholesome talk come out of your mouths, but only what is helpful for building others up according to their needs that it may benefit those who listen.

# *Battleground*

W̶hat have I told you? I will fight your battles for you. God has told us that, in his Word.

What do we do? We squirm, we cry, we whine that this isn't being done and that the enemy is tromping all over us. Whose fault is that? We forget. The battle is not won crying about it. We must fall to our knees and give praise to Him as the battle rages on. Remember Jehoshaphat? Years ago, when I was going through a bad period in my life I learned that verse. The battle belongs to the Lord. It helped me more that once when I wanted to cast my own stones. It was hard but I learned to give it to the Lord. It made a better person out of me. Remember Jehovah Nissi he is waiting for you to call on him to do your battle. Raise your hands in surrender and let the Lord take over. Watch how your battle gets won. Put on your whole armor of God. (Ephesians 6:13)

## Joshua 1:9
Have I not commanded you? Be strong and courageous, Do not be terrified, do not be discouraged, for the Lord your God will be with you where ever you go.

# Trees and water

As psalms 1:3 says like a tree planted by water you will grow. It was time to leave, I fought and kicked I screamed silently to myself, I cried. I pretended that I did not hear the gentle nudging of my heavenly Father, He was trying to tell me it was time. I couldn't believe it would ever happen to me in church. I was in a small church; with an excellent minister, but for some reason the church was not growing. He taught a good word and I soaked it up like a sponge. I had led a small bible study, the church was 7 years old and I had been there for 6. I realized that the Lord was trying to tell me to get ready. Six months before I left, the signs were appearing, little stuff, but I didn't see it happening. Finally at Christmas time it happened. Hurting words were spoken to me. Worse the minister knew this and didn't say or do anything about it. I was crushed, devastated, hurt. I started to visit another church with a friend who was also thinking of leaving, I enjoyed the service but something was missing. I visited 2 or 3 times before I visited another church where another friend attended she was in the choir and had been there a number of years. The minister talked about not letting your perfume get spoiled by dead flies. My decision was made in that split second. I started attending that church, become a member after the mandatory wait for six months and got baptized again. Now like a tree planted by water I began to flourish again. The drought was over my leaves are green and growing. I have grown to a higher level in my faith walk and have found new joy beyond belief. I could have saved myself the grief if only I had

41

listened to that small still voice earlier.

**Ecclesiastes 10:1**
As dead flies give perfume a bad smell, so a little folly outweighs wisdom and honor.

**1Corinthians 13:11**
When I was a child, I talked like a child, I thought like a child, I reasoned like a child. When I became a man I put childish ways behind me.

# *Pursue Your Purpose*

*R*ecently I changed churches and with the transition I was still feeling the effect of the newness, and unfamiliarity of it all. One of the first Sundays, though, the pastor taught on pursing your purpose. I have had the dream for years to write poetry and devotionals to my Lord Jesus. Letting other needs come first had sidetracked me, I was not using the gift that I had been blessed with. My mind was cluttered with things that I should have turned over to Him to take care of. I never let got of my purpose though I just always sidetracked it. What a sobering and sad thought that Sunday when he taught on that subject. He put me right where I needed to be, to pursue my purpose and to take that step of faith. He said that was our time. In Ephesians, Paul says we are chosen by God and through Christ have an inheritance. We are predestined to fulfill the purpose of God. We need to pursue every talent that God has placed inside of us, and with the aid of the Holy Spirit (our teacher) we can turn our talents into gifts that will bring honor and glory to God.

My pastor mentioned that Abraham pursued it; Dave pursued it now it is our time to pursue our passions and purposes. Remember only you can make that choice to pursue your purpose. To reach your goal.

**1 Corinthians 9:24**
do you not know that in a race all the runners run, but only one gets the prize? Run in such a way as to get the prize.

## Philippians 3:14

I press on toward the goal to win the prize for what God has called me heavenward in Christ Jesus.

# Silent wind chimes

They hang silently behind a screen and only when a stiff breeze comes along do you hear them tingle and sing. When you hear them, they produce melodious sounds. The various chimes have different songs they sing. The coppers, the heavy glass, the tubular ones, all produce their harmonious music only after the wind really blows and conquers the screen shielding them. The ones outside have the freedom to sway at the slightest breeze. Imagine the wind of the spirit being stifled because we do not allow him the freedom to move in our lives. Whether it is ignorance or fear, let the Holy Spirit take control. We, in our spiritual life sometimes put up the screen between the Holy Spirit and ourselves, even in some churches; they hamper the working of the Holy Spirit. Just think what would happen if we allowed the Holy Spirit full access at all times. Its time for the spirit to be given more freedom in our lives and churches.

**John 3:8**
The wind blows wherever it pleases. You hear it's sound, but you cannot tell where it comes from or where it is going. So it is with everyone born of the Spirit

# Who's watching you?

Talking with a friend I asked if she was still doing her morning devotional every morning. She said no she didn't have time with being pregnant, having morning sickness, still working every-day at a stressful job, a husband in graduate school and on top of that he had the flu all that week. I was disappointed at her response of "being too busy." Later as I was reflecting on the conversation, it occurred to me, what if God were too busy to watch over us for a day or even an hour. What a sobering though. The world would be in utter chaos. It says in scripture that He will never leave us nor forsake us. I am glad about that aren't you?

**Psalm 20:7**
Some trust in chariots and some in horses, but we trust in the name of the Lord or God.

**Matthew 6:28**
And why do you worry about clothes? See how the lilies of the field grow?

**Matthew 6: 31**
So do not worry about what shall I eat or what shall we drink? or what shall we wear?

# The Vine

*J*ohn 15 seems to be in everything I have read lately. My pastor did a series on abiding in the vine. A closer look at my life and reading verse 3 that says "you are already clean." Jesus was telling his disciples that he had pruned them already, the word prunes in Greek means clean. When I prune our hibiscus plants the look neater, cleaner and less out of control; if they are not taken care of and pruned they look scraggly and woody.

After pruning, they grow back with even more buds and flowers. Let Jesus work on you; let him, prune that dead wood off you and those dead leaves. Once pruned you will flower and bear much fruit. Orange trees when they are blossom emit a sweet perfume, but as the blooms begin to die they emit a foul odor. (Is3: 24 the first part) So lets not be like a dead fly giving off a bad scent. Let the Gardner, who is Jesus trim, fertilize, and take care of us so we can become like a sweet perfume when we bloom and bear fruit.

**2 Peter 3:18**
but grow in the grace and knowledge of our Lord and Savior Jesus Christ

# The spider web

I try to avoid spiders at all cost. They are not my favorite insects, and walking into a web is horrible. It stays with me all day long! As I walked around my yard early one morning, the fog was starting to dissipate and I saw this big spider web. This was no normal web. The filigree lace of the design as he was spinning it was incredible. I watched in fascination as the dew clung to the web almost like diamonds sparkling in the early morning sunlight. As I walked away I realized that, that web would be used to catch that spiders meals. Beauty for me to see. A trap to catch insects for the spider. How intricate God works his insects for catching food and giving us a moment of beauty at the same time.

**Genesis 1:24**
And God said, "let the land produce living creatures according to their kinds; livestock, creatures that move along the ground, and wild animals according to its kind.

# Garden by the Sea

♕

The garden by the sea boasts of wild flowers in many colors; yellow like sunflowers, pink in delicate hues, some fuchsia, and pale purple. In the wild undergrowth you can find them as you walk along the sandy shore, just steps away from the water. You can find the golden sea oats that help control the sand. All that is part of God's plan, the sea oats, flowers and the wild undergrowth, even the bothersome sandspurs. You have to wonder if the wide variety of flowers has anything to do with the scars in our hearts. Since flowers are delicate like our hearts, they get trampled on and broken. The Master Gardner who is also the Master Physician can fix them all. Psalm 23:3 says "He restores my soul" Just as he cares for and numbers the lilies that grow in the filed so to he knows everything about us even numbering the hairs on our head.

**Psalm 34:18**
The Lord is close to the broken hearted and saves those who are crushed in spirit.

# *Seasons*

You know the seasons of our lives
Autumn leaves turning brown, grass dies.
The flowers are gone from summer.
A sense of ending.
Winter is cold, barren, unloving.
We try to grasp what our situations are.
We feel a loss that we cannot comprehend.
The winter winds buffet us to and fro. We know we must hold on.
Spring!
Life has returned. Spiritually we have awakened.
Our Jesus does love us.
We prune back the old dead branches.
We fertilize for growth.
Gentle spring rains arrive.
John 15:6 says to abide in Him for continued growth.
Summer is full of blossoms on shrubs, trees, and flowers.
The growth in all of God's glory.
The sweet perfume of all the flowers
All like the sweet perfume of Jesus.
Remember the season you are in will not last forever.
The season of growth will return.

**Colossians 1:10**
And we pray this in order that you may live a life worthy of the
Lord and may please him in every way; bearing fruit in every good

work growing in the knowledge of God.

### Ecclesiastes 3:1
There is a time for everything, and a season for every activity under heaven.

# Steady Rain

*D*on't you love a soft steady rain? The kind where you just want to kick back, stay home from work and close your eyes and imagine? The rain slowly seeping into your heart, the Word of God. Cutting through all the layers of dirt, rock and clay clods that are stubborn. Slowly seeping in, Finally reaching the rich dark soil untouched by anything. Ping, ping. Thirsty soil soaking in the rain. Ping; ping soaking into your heart. God slowly awakens the sleeping child within with his seeds of love planted years ago. Ping ping. The seed starts to grow, a maturity comes about the living streams of water flowing forth. The growth of the seed will produce the most wondrous fragrant flower of all.

**John 7:38**
Whoever believes in me, as the scripture has said, streams of living water will flow from within him

# Struggling Sunrise

Clouds rushing past as the night leaves the sky. Brilliant streaks of pink are already painted, the pale orange appearing through the gray distant horizon meeting the sea. To my left sheets of rain are pouring down. The sky is divided. A mighty struggle is taking place. Blue has broken through. The window has opened. The constant wind sweeping through the clouds. A paintbrush painting the ever changing colors. The rain has now moved in front of the horizon another sheet of rain is following behind. Look on the horizon says the Lord, have patience. You are so focused on one area you are not noticing the pink struggling to come through, struggling just like you, when you have a problem: you only see one area of it. Colors so vast they have no names, other than being called a shade of peach, or pink, are hiding the sunrise. The low dark rain clouds have marched in again across the sky, it is now raining. Look to your left, white sky has broken thru. The sky is now divided into squall lines and sunrise. The wind, constant, like the wind of the spirit trying to break into our minds, telling us to listen. God is with us at all times. As another low dark cloud has appeared moving across the ever-changing horizon, I am sure if I move to the railing I will get very wet. The rain has won. A mighty struggle has taken place; God has shown His magnificent power.

**Ephesians 6:12**
For our struggle is not against flesh and blood, but against the rulers, against the authorities, against the powers of this dark world

and against the spiritual forces of evil in the heavenly realms.

**Luke 8:25**
..In fear and amazement they asked one another, "Who is this? He commands even the winds and the water, and they obey him."

# Dancing Rainbows

God never ceases to amaze me. Leaning over the rail of our cruise ship. I was watching the waves go by, frothy and foamy, they were white on the turquoise blue of the Pacific Ocean. My husband was taking pictures of the island that we were passing and said, "Hey look at that!" What was I supposed to look at? Dancing rainbows. Amazingly as the sun hit the waves, there were dancing rainbows inside of them. As quickly as they appeared they disappeared. This happened for a few minutes then I guess the sun was in the wrong direction. What a wonderful place for rainbows to be. Another present from God. A reminder of his everlasting covenant of love for us as he surrounds us with his gifts for us to enjoy. Click a snapshot from God.

**Job 38:33**
Do you know the laws of heavens?

**Ecclesiastes 3:11**
He has made everything beautiful in its time.

# Cloud show

*B*efore dawn a cloud cover inches closer to the full moon, just skirting the edges. The moon glow spills on the clouds, creating a silver edging. As dawn creeps over the horizon the sunrise starts it's show. Rain clouds close by hide any sunrise extravaganza. A few sprinkles on the windshield on the way to work. Rain clouds to the east-southeast. Clouds, and rain. You can see where the rain has been falling. Light diffuses all different colors as the sun rises and the rain clouds dance together in almost perfect harmony. From dirty gray clouds to almost steel black, now white clouds to just an off white, and all of this in a partly sunny sky. Now that I have arrived at work, I have a beautiful blue sky with a brilliant shining sun. All of this in just a thirty minute drive from home to work. Even though I don't know the names of the clouds other than what I learned in school, nimbus, cumulus, and cirrus. I call them a work of art from God. Just another gift for us to enjoy. Another snapshot from God.

**Psalm 8:3**
When I consider your heavens, .....

**Psalm 147:8**
He covers the sky with clouds; he supplies the earth with rain and makes grass grow on the hills.

# Your Prayer Closet

*L*istening to a speaker on the radio, she mentioned how before she was scheduled to speak at a conference she wanted a quiet place to pray. She went to the ladies room, it was quiet and she was able to pray and seek God's word before she spoke. While waiting for my grandson to be born, I could not find any place that was really quiet and still close enough. The waiting area was very noisy with kids, people and a loud television, and the gift shop was right there also. I slipped into the ladies room to pray, I apologized to God for praying there but it was the only quiet place. I prayed for a few minutes and went back to the waiting area. I am sure not even ten minutes went by before my son in law came running down the hall to say our grandson had arrived. It doesn't matter where you pray and I am sure that speaker and I have not been the only ones to seek God in the ladies room! I pray in the shower, while doing dishes and while hanging my clothes out even cooking dinner. What matters is that we seek Him in everything we do. He will meet us wherever we are. Matthew 28:20. All we have to do is ask.

**Psalm 27:8**
My hearts says of you, "Seek his face!" Your face, Lord will I seek.

**Joshua 5:15**
the commander of the Lord's army replied, "take off your sandals, for the place where you are standing is holy.

# Foggy Mornings

When Morning fog hides the sun I call it white sun. Some might even call it eerie.

Fog, a mysterious shroud of mist that hides our sins. Surrounding everything around. When we do things we know we shouldn't, we like to think we are hiding from God. Hiding in the fog. Hiding like Adam and Eve in the garden. As the sun starts to rise, the brighter it gets the more fog it burns off. It is just like God burning off the dross to refine us. The brighter the sun the clearer the sky and before you know it, the fog is gone. I love to watch it as it goes from not being there to seeing to a bright ball of fire. That is the way it is with God. He puts us in the fire to burn the dross off to make us pure and to shine in his light

**Isaiah 1:25**
I will turn my hand against you: I will thoroughly purge away your dross and remove your impurities.

**Psalm 51:10**
Create in me a pure heart, O God, and renew a steadfast spirit it me.

# Hurricane

Apprehension, expectation the winds are starting to blow. Blowing from one direction to another never ceasing. In a whirlwind, in the eye I find comfort, the calm of my Lord. So let the north winds blow chilly and cold. Let the south wind blow warm and inviting. Apprehension and expectations are ways of life for us. Always wanting good but expecting bad. Always trying to stay calm in the eye of the storm. But, there your lord waits. Let him calm you with his love, embrace you with his arms. Let the north wind blow and howl as you are comforted in the eye let the south wind blow balmy and breezy everything will be all right. North, South, East, West. As far is the east is from the west. Your Lord will see you through for He has said he will never forsake you. (Hebrews 13:5)

**Psalm 16:8**
I have set the Lord always before me. Because he is at my right hand, I will not be shaken.

**Song of Solomon 4:16**
Awake, north wind, and come south wind!

# Sunset Distraction

*T*he people all around me made such a distraction. You had to wonder why they were there, if it wasn't to enjoy the beautiful Florida sunset. We had driven to Captiva Island to watch the sunset; all around the people were talking. As they talked and carried on about stuff, I sat on the sand and watched the sky as it took on the marvelous colors of God. His paint palette always has new colors on it! Mauve, purple, muted pinks, a cloudbank teasing the sun, tangerine orange as it slowly sank into a split cloudbank, now you see it now you don't, as the evening clouds turned the color of the sun into a deeper color, more awesome than ever. Just how many of those people really appreciated the gift they had witnessed ? Artwork from God! I tried to tune them all out as I silently sat in awe of this masterpiece, thanking God that I could be there to see it. Just like our spiritual eyes, they need to be opened to your very being so we can see your beauty. Take away the stress that so many carry around with them and allow them a moment of peace and love with you. After that, they will never be the same.

**Colossians 3:15**
Le the peace of Christ rule in your hearts, since as members of one body you were called to peace.

# Junk Mail

Notice how many things are generic now days? Nothing is ever personal any more. Generic food, computerized voices on the phone, a voice that says: we have an important message for you, please hold the line? Now that is real junk. Even the clerks in the stores are so self-centered they can't say thank you with your name. Even our junk mail is addressed as postal patron. There is one place though where our name is written. As a matter of fact it is written three times! The lambs book of life Rev 21:27. The white stone with our name on it Rev 2:17, and Is 49:16 where it says that our name is inscribed on the palm of His hand What does that tell us about our God? We are very personal to him. He even knows the number of hairs on our head. We are his sheep and he calls us by name. John 10:3

**Is. 43:1**
But now this is what the Lord say's he who created you, O Jacob he who formed you, O Israel: Fear not for I have redeemed you; I have summoned you by name; you are mine.

# Got Jesus

*L*istening to two women talk one day at lunch I over heard one say she had eaten at a new restaurant the night before and had enjoyed it. A barbeque place that was excellent. The other woman she was talking to said "oh I liked it when it was the other place" meaning an Italian restaurant. Although she hadn't eaten there yet her opinion was formed in the negative. How many of us are like that. Not willing to give something new a try?

We think if we come to Jesus that our lives won't be fun any more and we will have to be straight laced and gloomy.

Oh but when we come to Him we have the time of our lives as he takes us on a roller coaster ride we will never forget. Exhilarating, breathtaking. Everyday a new adventure.

Try Jesus you will like him.

**Matthew 18:3**
And he said: I tell you the truth, unless you change and become like little children, you will never enter the kingdom of heaven.

# Leftovers

*I* love leftovers!!! They are wonderful! Especially chili, pasta salad, anything that has a marinade in it tastes so much better the next day. The spices mingle and it gets better. Some food should never be saved, as leftovers, they taste awful, like sliced apples or oranges! The Israelites had this problem, they wanted leftovers. They tried to save their manna it did not work. Mold appeared on it and they had to throw it away. They wanted to make sure they ate. On weekends they gathered double as instructed and God kept it good for them. There are also people who don't do leftovers. Neither does God. His laws are very specific regarding this. First fruits of everything; Tithing, giving of your time, giving to your favorite charity. This is just some of your first fruits.

**Exodus 23:19**
Bring the best of your firstfruits of your soil to the house of the Lord your God.

# Quiet Sunset

*A*s we walked onto the beach in the early evening the waves were gently lapping the shore as low tide was coming in. The flocks of different kinds of shore birds were on the sand bars feeding. As I was able to get close to them, I noticed the different marking on all of them and all the different varieties. Some of them had orange rings on their beaks, others had white polka dots on their black tail feathers!!! Sometimes they stood with one leg up in the air as if the sand were tickling their webbed feet! As I took another step, they whooshed away. The fluttering of their wings swooshing by, only to land on another sand bar to finish feeding. Looking to the west, the sun was in a window frame surrounded by gray rain clouds. To the left you could already see the lighthouse flashing. Only a couple of minutes more.

Then the window shade was pulled down and the sun had set for the evening.

As I waded in the shallow water I reflected that even though there had been no spectacular sunset to speak of, the beauty of God was all around me. The variety of birds that I would not have otherwise paid attention to, the beauty of the split second sunset and the awe of the quiet as the early evening started to set in, what a beautiful evening after all.

**1 Kings 19:12**
After the earthquake came a fire, but the Lord was not in the fire. And after the fire came a gentle whisper.

# *Floundering in the dark*

One time my husband and I went to the beach to see the sunset. We hadn't gone to that particular beach very often, so when we decided to walk back to the car we got lost! We missed our pathway marker. The afterglow was gone and it was dark. We had gotten turned around. So we just walked until we found some light. We cut between some condos and found a sidewalk. We did not know where we were walking, only toward the light. Afterward, I associated that evening with my walk with Jesus. We flounder in the dark, turning every way but toward the light. The fear sets in because we don't see any light to go toward, once we see the light of Jesus we will never be in the dark again.

**Psalm 119:105**
Your word is a lamp unto my feet and a light for my path

**Psalm 27:1**
The Lord is my light and my salvation whom shall I fear?

# God's Song

Walking in the gently crashing waves
I hear God softly singing to me.
His voice is in the waves,
The bird's overhead, the pelicans as they dive.
Clouds as they race across the sky.
Shoes in hand.
Toes sinking in the sand.
God delighting in me rejoicing in me
Laughing at me (His child!!)
As the sand tickles my toes.
Rolling waves tumbling down the beach,
Crashing upon each other.
The melody goes on and on
As God thrills me with his love and quiets me with his song.

**Zephaniah 3:17**
The Lord your God is with you,
He is mighty to save.
He will take great delight in you,
He will quiet you with his love, he will rejoice over you with
singing

# Calico Kitten

Curled up on a bed of soft pine needles he lays sleeping so tenderly just like a baby. Completely off guard. He is a baby kitten, calico in color. I have never seen him sleeping before, I always see him in action, trotting in from the field or from across the street where he has been hunting. With his beautiful, inquiring eyes he scampers to the door to see if I am going to feed him and the rest of the gang. Meaning another golden cat with white paws and two others deep golden in color. He has gotten to be very friendly with me. I think I have even heard his little motor purring on the accidental occasion he let me pick him up. It startled him as much as it startled me! Can't hold him for too long, he has to get down. He is learning that I will not hurt him. He is learning to trust me. Sometimes it takes a long time acquire the trust of a person. Even after that, that person can still hurt your feelings. Then that trust has to be reestablished all over again. When friends do that with stinging words, that breaks some of the friend ship and trust. With knowing Jesus, we go thru the same thing; we learn to trust Jesus with everything. He knows what is best for us even when we think we know what we want. He says for us to take his yoke because it is light and easy to bear. Trust in Jesus today.

**Hebrew 2:13**
And again I will put my trust in Him and again behold I and the children, which God hath given me.

**Psalm 56:3**
When I am afraid, I will trust in you.

# Covenant Promise

*T*he rainbow is the covenant promise of God's love for us. As I saw the rainbow dip into the Gulf of Mexico a portion of it disappeared from our sight as a gray cloud drifted past it. Suddenly, looking up, we saw the brilliance of the rainbow again as it sat on a backdrop of a brilliant white thunderhead cloud, the purple and red of the rainbow showing the magnificent colors. Racing gray clouds kept covering over the rainbow. We would see it show up again in different areas of the cloud. Rainbow, gray clouds, rainbow. That is the way our lives are. Sometimes God's love is shown is such magnitude and other times we wonder where He is when things go sour for us and all we see are the gray clouds. Just remember that He is always there, even when the colors of the rainbow aren't. For He has said he will never leave us or forsake us.

**Genesis 9:11**
I establish my covenant with you: never again will all life be cut off by the waters of a flood; never again will there be a flood to destroy the earth.

# The Lilies

*B*rowse means to feed upon, to gaze. Browse among the lilies. As I was studying the Book of the Song of Solomon the word browse struck me, I needed to look it up. The meaning surprised me. Day lilies are beautiful when they bloom, they come in a variety of colors. The most striking ones are red and white. They bloom in the springtime. My mom planted them to have some color in the field when she lived with us. She enjoyed them so much. The word of God is the same way. We gaze upon our bibles ready to feed on the word of God. At first it sometimes intimidates us, the smallness of the print, the aspect of so many words, the different books in it. We browse the word; we gaze upon the word, as we as we continue to study it, we come to feed upon it. Eventually it becomes our morning meal.

**John 6:27**
Do not work for food that spoils, but for food that endures to eternal life, which the Son of man will give you.

**Proverbs 1:5**
Let the wise listen and add to their learning, and let the discerning get guidance.

# Glacier Bay

*N*ot knowing what to expect as we sailed into Glacier Bay I was in total awe.

I am sure my mouth dropped open at the exquisite beauty. The morning fog had finally cleared off and our ship was slowly inching into the bay as a struggling sun was starting to shine. It was going to be a beautiful day after all. The majestic mountains with pine trees growing on them, the mountain peaks topped with snow, wild flowers blooming and the ever-flowing streams coming down from the peaks. Where else can you find such beauty? As we continued to cruise we came upon the mountainous glaciers in their pure crystalline blue color, with the occasional thunder telling us that a glacier had calved. (A breaking off of a larger glacier). I had often wondered how they got that blue in the pictures that I saw in travel brochures and magazines, Coming face to face with a glacier larger than our ship assured me that the color was real. The descriptions of a glacier can only be described best as beautiful. You have to see them to believe them, the ice floes with the harp seals were picture perfect shots. The chunks of ice flowing out to sea completing the cycle, snow to ice, back to water again. Our first trip to Glacier Bay, Alaska will be forever remembered for its beauty of God etched in my mind.

**Job 37:5**
God's voice thunders in marvelous ways; He does great things beyond our understanding.

# Jealousy

♔

You wouldn't think that God could be as jealous as he is. How many times do you feel the tugging to just get away to listen to worship music or read your bible or just be in the silence of His Presence? How many times do you wake up in the middle of the night praying? How many times have you said not now, I'm busy? I'll get alone with God later and later never comes? We are always putting God in second place; after we do dishes, watch a favorite TV show, take out the garbage. Isn't it time to put God first in your life I find that if I do not have my quiet time with Him, it is like I haven't had my morning cup of coffee. He is a jealous God and wants none before Him. The book of Exodus tells us that in chapter 20:3. Do not put anything before him because he is a jealous God.

**1Corinthins 10:22**
Are we trying to arouse the Lord's jealousy?

# *Walk*

*D*oes our walk match our talk? We can talk as much as we want about being saved. We might even go to church attend Sunday school maybe even Bible Study classes but does our walk match our talk? Scripture speaks of being ready to spread the Word. We can have all the knowledge we want, but it needs to be spread. How are we supposed to spread it?? By word of mouth and by our feet is the way. It is also a command from Jesus as He was leaving this earth to go back home to heaven. Go yea into all the nations Mark 16:15. Wherever we go we should spread the word by our actions, words, deeds and smiles, so that there is no question that we are children of God. "Order our steps oh Lord." Isaiah in his book says how lovely are the feet of those who bring the gospel. Share the word of God today.

**Ephesians 6:15**
and with your feet fitted with the readiness that comes from the gospel of peace.

**Psalm 119:133**
Direct my footsteps according to your word, let no sin rule over me

# *Road Signs*

When we go on road trips we follow a map or a road atlas. These help us to find our way to our destination. When the people of Judah were finally able to find their way back they used the guidepost that they had set up when they were led out of the land. Now they were able to find their way back to Judah. We follow the road signs to keep us in the right directions, to let us know when we can get gas, a place to sleep, something to eat. It is the same thing in the Bible God sets up guideposts and markers for us to find the way to his heart and when we follow directions we can't get lost. Chapters 30 and 31 in Jeremiah tell of the restoration of Israel. Isaiah 35 says it wonderfully, the way of holiness if we follow the road signs we will make it to our destination.

**Jeremiah 31:21**
Set up road signs; put up guideposts. Take note of the highway,the road that you take.

**Isaiah 35:8**
and a highway will be there: it will be called the Way of Holiness. The unclean will not journey on it; it will be for those who walk in that Way; wicked fools will not go about on it.

# Saturday Disciples

Waiting one Saturday morning for my friends to arrive to have breakfast together I looked around the restaurant. What I observed was a variety of people all around.

Some were not speaking English but talking very animated with their hands, others in intense conversation not noticing any else around, others laughing and having a good time enjoying their food.

Some were waiting like me. This reminded me of the disciples when Jesus called them and they all followed him. We are all different, just like they were. There was Peter there was Matthew, Judas who handled the money, and Thomas who doubted Jesus. Everyday we are like one of the disciples. Some days we are like Peter we are ready to do anything for Jesus until the time comes. Some days we are like the other disciples wondering if Jesus is there and sometimes doubting it. Sadly some are like Judas who will forsake Jesus for earthly pleasures. John the beloved we don't hear much about, except how much he loved his Master. When we follow Jesus we will have real joy. Look around today and watch people; you can tell what kind they are by their continence. Real joy on their faces, or a mask of happiness. What are they missing?

The answer: they are missing Jesus. Is your face showing the love of Jesus in your life?

**Matthew 4:19**
" Come, follow me, Jesus said " and I will make you fishes of men.'

**Psalm 34:1, 5**

I will extol the Lord at all times; His praise will always be on my lips, Those who look to Him are radiant; their faces are never covered with shame.

# The Classroom

$\mathcal{A}$s the Holy Spirit leads the class, we never know where he is going to take us in our study. In the morning I have a devotional that I study and I follow the verse that they recommend and sometimes that leads to another theme. Thinking we are going to have a dry study, the Holy Spirit might take us on a study that you would not believe. We will be wishing we had more time than our so called designated study time, before we have to get ready for our workday. In ten to fifteen minutes you can fill a page of paper and go to as many scriptures that you can find. With the Holy Spirit as our teacher and counselor we will learn as much as we can handle. He only asks one thing of us, to be serious and to use what we learn in the word. Not to hoard our learning. Not to hide our light under the bushel basket.

**Proverbs I: 5**
let the wise listen and add to their learning, and let the discerning get guidance.

**Isaiah 50:4 .**
He wakens me morning by morning, wakens my ear to listen like one being taught.

# Knock, knock

Not long ago I had to have an MRI, The technician gave me earplugs because of
the noise that I would hear. She told me that at various times I would hear this knocking. As the machine started I heard it, Knock, knock. Knock. Knock, knock. There was nothing on the inside. The thought occurred to that, that machine reminded me of the picture of Jesus, where he is knocking on a door without a doorknob. It has to be opened from the inside. Basically it reminded me that Jesus is always knocking at our hearts for us to let him in. In the book of Revelation it says," Here I am!" The invitation is there. Won't you let him into your heart today?

**Matthew 7:7**
Ask and it will be given to you, seek and you shall find: Knock and the door will be opened to you

If you have never made a commitment to Jesus as your Lord and savior, if you are looking to fill that empty place inside you that nothing in this world can fill and if this book has touched you, if you would like Jesus to be the Lord of your Life it's simple. The word of God says in **Romans 10:9** that if you confess with your mouth, Jesus is Lord, and believe in your heart that God raised him from the dead you will be saved.

Now go and tell someone. Jesus really does love you!

Printed in the United States
18925LVS00004B/145-1008